AF599581

CANE CORSO

BY CORINNE FICKETT

TABLE OF CONTENTS

A Crabtree Seedlings Book

Crabtree Publishing
crabtreebooks.com

School-to-Home Support for Caregivers and Teachers

This book helps children grow by letting them practice reading. Here are a few guiding questions to help the reader with building his or her comprehension skills. Possible answers appear here in red.

Before Reading:

- What do I think this book is about?
  - *I think this book is about Cane Corsos.*
  - *I think this book is about bully breeds.*
- What do I want to learn about this topic?
  - *I want to learn about a Cane Corso's behavior.*
  - *I want to know why a Cane Corso is a bully breed.*

During Reading:

- I wonder why...
  - *I wonder why Cane Corsos are very protective of their owners.*
  - *I wonder why Cane Corsos are so big.*
- What have I learned so far?
  - *I have learned that Cane Corsos have muscular bodies.*
  - *I have learned that Cane Corsos can weigh more than 100 pounds (45 kg).*

After Reading:

- What details did I learn about this topic?
  - *I have learned that Cane Corsos are very smart.*
  - *I have learned that bully breeds come from Molosser dogs.*
- Read the book again and look for the vocabulary words.
  - *I see the word breed on page 3, and the word muscular on page 4. The other glossary words are found on pages 22 and 23.*

The Cane Corso is a bully **breed**.

Tibetan Mastiffs

All bully breeds come from Molosser dogs. These dogs were large and **muscular**.

FUN FACT

Molosser dogs came from Greece.

Cane Corsos have muscular bodies, like other bully breeds.

They also have **broad** chests.

Their coat is short, **stiff**, and shiny.

Many Cane Corsos are a solid color such as black or gray. Some are **brindle**.

Most Cane Corsos weigh 90 to 110 pounds (41 to 50 kilograms). They stand 23 to 28 inches (58 to 71 centimeters) tall.

FUN FACT

A Cane Corso's average life span is 9 to 12 years.

These dogs are gentle and loving. They enjoy being with their owners.

Cane Corsos are very smart and like to learn. They are very **protective** of their owners and homes.

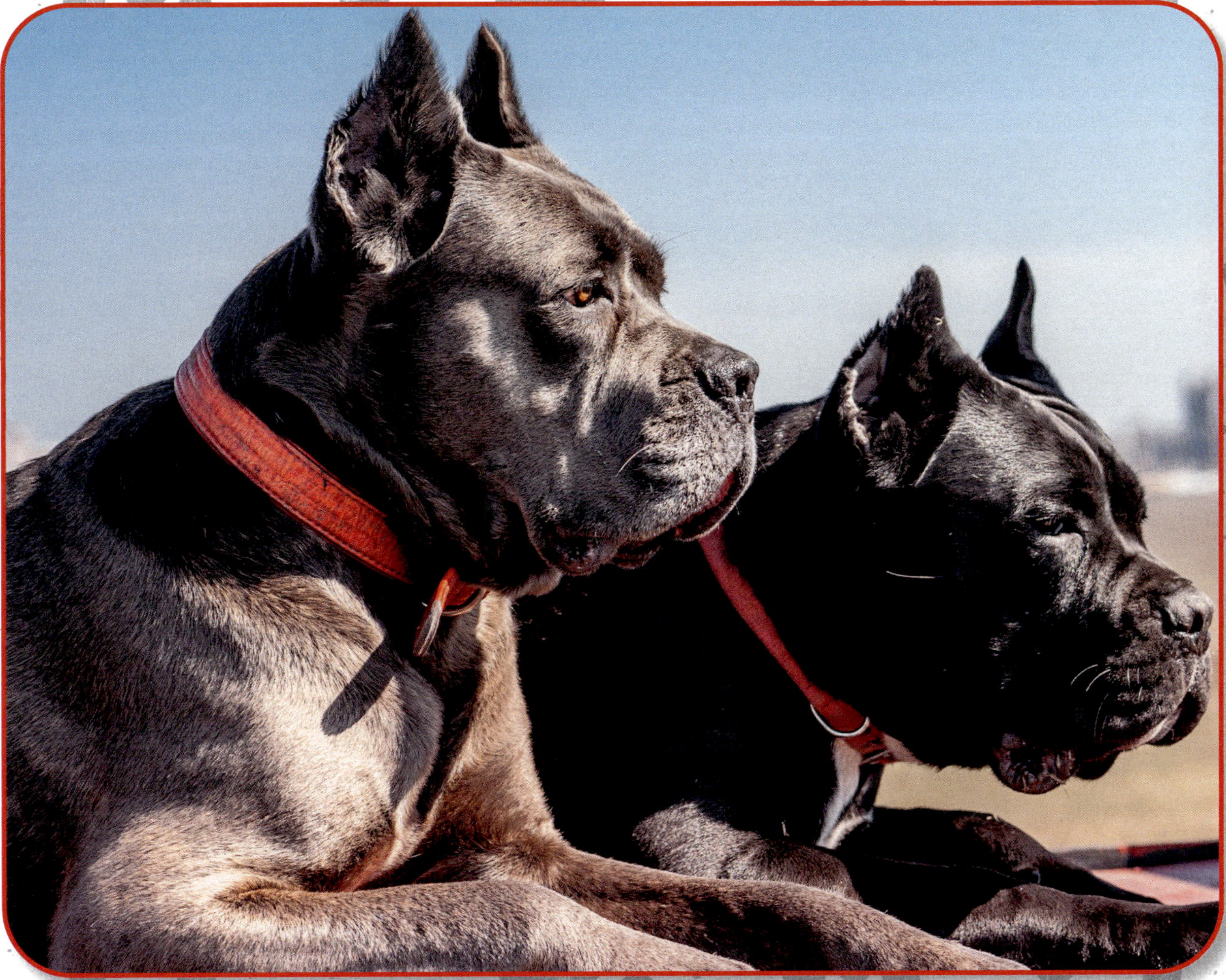

FUN FACT

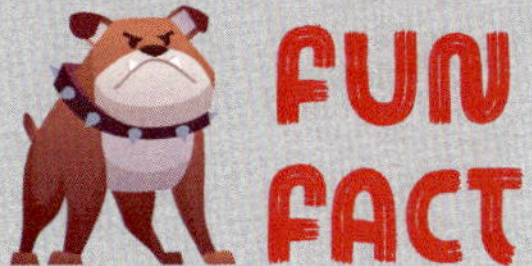

Cane Corso roughly translates to "bodyguard" in Latin.

NBA player Devin Booker owns a Cane Corso named Haven.

Cane Corsos are athletic. They enjoy being active.

A Cane Corso can be a great addition to the right family.

Am I Ready to Adopt a Dog?

Adopting a dog is a big responsibility. It is important for you and your family to be fully prepared and committed to providing the best possible care for your furry friend. Take this quiz to see if you and your family are ready to talk about getting a dog.

1. Do you know that dogs require a lot of attention and care? **Yes / No**
2. Are you willing to spend time playing, walking, and interacting with a dog every day? **Yes / No**
3. Do you understand that dogs need regular feeding, grooming, and visits to the veterinarian? **Yes / No**
4. Are you patient enough to train a dog and teach them basic commands like sit, stay, and come? **Yes / No**
5. Is your household free of dog allergies? **Yes / No**
6. Do you have enough space in your home and an area for a dog to move around and play? **Yes / No**
7. Can you commit to caring for a dog for its entire life span? **Yes / No**
8. Are you prepared to clean up after the dog, including picking up its poop? **Yes / No**
9. Can you handle the financial responsibility of providing food, toys, medical care, and other necessities for the dog? **Yes / No**
10. Do you understand that dogs need regular socialization with other dogs and people to stay happy and well-behaved? **Yes / No**
11. Are you willing to commit to taking care of a dog during busy times or vacations? **Yes / No**
12. Can you handle the challenges of training and caring for a dog, even when things get tough? **Yes / No**

Determine your score by adding up all the "yes" answers.

10-12 Yes answers: You are ready to begin a conversation about adopting a dog.
6-9 Yes answers: You might be ready to think about adopting a dog.
0-5 Yes answers: You are not ready to take on the huge responsibility of adopting a furry friend.

Myths About Bully Breeds

Myth 1

Bully breeds are the most dangerous types of dogs.

Studies have not found that bully breeds are more dangerous than other types of dogs. The American Veterinary Medical Association (AVMA) states that any dog can bite. A dog's individual history and situation determines how likely it is to bite.

Myth 2

Bully breeds can lock their jaws.

No dog breed is able to "lock" its jaws. Usually, larger dogs have stronger bites than smaller dogs.

Myth 3

Bully breeds are more aggressive than other dogs.

Any dog can show aggression. Research shows that aggression is not breed specific. A dog's behavior usually comes from how it is brought up, cared for, and trained.

Myth 4

Bully breeds are cute.

Bully breeds are not just cute—they are adorable! They bring joy to their families.

Glossary

breed (breed): A group of animals, within a species, that share specific physical characteristics

brindle (BRIN-dl): A pattern on an animal's coat that has colored streaks or stripes, especially in shades of brown and gray

broad (brawd): Wide from side to side

muscular (MUHS-kyuh-ler): Having strong, well-developed muscles. Muscles are body parts that help a person or animal move.

protective (pruh-TEK-tiv): Able or showing a strong wish to keep others safe from danger

stiff (stif): Hard and difficult to bend or change shape

Index

About the Author

Corinne Fickett lives in Taos, New Mexico with her husband and seven rescue dogs. She enjoys hiking in the desert and painting watercolor landscapes. Her favorite dessert is vanilla ice cream topped with chocolate syrup and rainbow sprinkles.

Written by: Corinne Fickett
Designed by: Kathy Walsh
Series Development: James Earley
Proofreader: Janine Deschenes
Educational Consultant: Marie Lemke M.Ed.

Photographs: All images from Shutterstock. p 11, 12, 21 K Cemelli

Crabtree Publishing

crabtreebooks.com 800-387-7650

Copyright © 2025 Crabtree Publishing

All rights reserved. No part of this publication may be reproduced, stored in a retrieval system or be transmitted in any form or by any means, electronic, mechanical, photocopying, recording, or otherwise, without the prior written permission of Crabtree Publishing.

In Canada: We acknowledge the financial support of the Government of Canada through the Canada Book Fund for our publishing activities.

Printed in the USA/062024/CG20240201

Published in Canada
Crabtree Publishing
616 Welland Avenue
St. Catharines, Ontario
L2M 5V6

Published in the United States
Crabtree Publishing
347 Fifth Avenue
Suite 1402-145
New York, New York, 10016

Library and Archives Canada Cataloguing in Publication
Available at Library and Archives Canada

Library of Congress Cataloging-in-Publication Data
Available at the Library of Congress

Hardcover: 978-1-0398-4472-8
Paperback: 978-1-0398-4553-4
Ebook (pdf): 978-1-0398-4626-5
Epub: 978-1-0398-4696-8
Read-Along: 978-1-0398-4766-8
Audio: 978-1-0398-4836-8